WHAT GOOD IS A TAIL?

DOROTHY HINSHAW PATENT

PHOTOGRAPHS BY
WILLIAM MUÑOZ

COBBLEHILL BOOKS / Dutton

NEW YORK

For Elsa and Ninja,
whose happily wagging tails brighten my days.
D.H.P.

For Sandy — Thank you for your patience.
W.M.

ACKNOWLEDGMENTS

The author and photographer would like to thank the following people and institutions for their gracious help with this book: Lincoln Park Zoo in Chicago; Knoxville Zoo; National Bison Range; Busch Gardens in Tampa, Florida; Lowery Park Zoo in Tampa, Florida; Duke University Primate Center; Marine World Africa USA in Vallejo, California; the Montana Fish, Wildlife and Parks Department; Neil and Karin of the Wolf Scat Ranch; Arizona Sonora Desert Museum in Tucson, Arizona; Shedd Aquarium in Chicago; Phoenix Zoo; Barbara and Craig Candelaria; Cincinnati Zoo; Aransas National Wildlife Refuge; Metcalf National Wildlife Refuge; Fossil Rim Wildlife Park in Glenrose, Texas; St. Louis Zoo; Sam ("the Reptile Man") Manno and Sandy Nicolet of Coral Sea Pets and Supplies, Missoula, Montana.

LIBRARY OF CONGRESS CATALOGING-IN-PUBLICATION DATA
Patent, Dorothy Hinshaw.
What good is a tail? / Dorothy Hinshaw Patent; photographs by William Muñoz.
p. cm.
Includes index.
Summary: Looks at various animal tails and their uses.
ISBN 0-525-65148-9
1. Tail—Juvenile literature. [1. Tail.] I. Muñoz, William, ill. II. Title.
QL950.6.P38 1994
596'.049—dc20 92-45639 CIP AC

Published in the United States by Cobblehill Books,
an affiliate of Dutton Children's Books, a division of Penguin Books USA, Inc.,
375 Hudson Street, New York, New York 10014

DESIGNED BY JOSEPH RUTT

Printed in Hong Kong   First Edition
10 9 8 7 6 5 4 3 2

CONTENTS

CHAPTER ONE
WHAT IS A TAIL?

Tails come in many shapes and sizes. There are short fat tails and long skinny ones. Some tails have no fur, others are fluffy. Some tails can curl up, others just seem to hang down.

A giraffe has a long skinny tail with a dark tuft at the end.

The rhinoceros curls its short tail when it runs.

LEFT: *Bears have very short tails.*

ABOVE: *Horses raise their tails when they run in excitement.*

RIGHT: *What we call a bird's tail is actually made up of feathers attached to a short true tail.*

But just what is a tail anyway? It's the part of the body that sticks out beyond the end of the digestive system. In animals with backbones, the spine reaches into the tail. These tails also have muscles for movement. Animals like horses have long hair on their tails. The hair hangs way down beyond the end. Some things we call tails actually aren't. If you eat "lobster tail," you aren't really eating the animal's tail. You are making a meal of a part of its body called the abdomen.

The actual tail of birds is very short. Bones are heavy, and a short tail means fewer weighty bones that would make flying difficult. What we call a bird's tail is made up of feathers carried by a short bit of spine.

ABOVE: *Captive elephants may be trained to "tail up," each one curling its trunk around the tail of the elephant ahead.*

LEFT: *Many animals, like these ring-tailed lemurs, use their tails to help support their bodies when they sit.*

Some tails are beautiful. Others appear strange to us. But however they look, tails can be very useful to animals. Tails show feelings. When they run excitedly, some animals hold their tails way up. Others twitch them or wag them back and forth.

Tails can be practical, too. Animals as different as lizards and some breeds of sheep store fat in their tails. That way, when there isn't enough food, they can live off the fat until they find food again. Animals with long bushy tails, like foxes and wolves, curl their tails protectively around their faces when they sleep.

This fox is sleeping with its tail wrapped protectively around its face.

CHAPTER TWO
GETTING AROUND

Tails are handy for getting around. They are especially useful in water. Just a gentle flick of the tail can push a fish smoothly along. Alligators have long, flattened tails for swimming. The alligator swings its tail slowly back and forth in the water as it glides silently forward, only its eyes and nose above the surface. The movement of the tail is so gentle that no ripples even show as the alligator swims. The flat, naked tail of the beaver is used as a paddle for swimming. When a beaver is alarmed, it slaps its tail on the surface of the water to warn nearby beavers of danger.

LEFT: *Fish, like this black-tipped shark, swim using their tails.*

RIGHT: *The alligator's tail is a powerful paddle for swimming.*

ABOVE: *Whales and their relatives, such as this beluga, use the flukes at the ends of their tails to power themselves through the water.*

RIGHT: *The tail muscles of dolphins are powerful enough to enable them to "stand on their tails" for the audience.*

BELOW: *Sea lions have very small tails.*

Whales and dolphins have special fins called flukes at the ends of their tails. The flukes are stroked up and down, powering the animal through the water. Seals and sea lions have almost no tail at all. Their hind legs have webbing between the toes of the back feet. When the sea lion swims, it strokes with its front flippers. It holds the hind flippers together behind it, bending them to steer like a tail. Seals swim using the hind flippers, stroking them in turn.

ABOVE: *Most ducks, like this male wood duck, have fairly short tails.*

BELOW: *Some parrots, like this macaw, have long tail feathers.*

When flying, birds use their tails for lift, steering, soaring, and braking. You can sometimes tell a lot about how a bird lives by looking at its tail. Birds with small tails, like ducks, fly mostly in the open. Without trees in the way, they can fly straight, so they don't need long tails. But forest birds, such as many parrots, use their longer tails to steer their way through the trees.

Tails are important to hunting birds, too. When hawks and eagles dive after prey, they make small adjustments of their tails to help keep them on target. Their tails are also spread when they soar, providing surface area that helps support their bodies in the air. Birds that must land on tree branches or nests brake their flight with their tails. Insect-eating birds like swallows and kites often have streamlined, v-shaped tails that help them zigzag swiftly through the air after their fast-moving prey.

14

Gulls use their tail feathers to help them soar and steer.

BELOW: An osprey brakes its flight with its tail as it lands on its nest.

15

The wallaby, a small kind of kangaroo, rests
on its tail while standing.

CHAPTER THREE
BALANCING AND HANGING ON

Tails are useful for balancing and hanging on. Woodpeckers have especially stiff tail feathers that they use to brace themselves against the trunk as they climb or drill into the tree with their beaks searching for insects.

Birds aren't the only animals that use their tails for support. Animals that run on two legs often have long, strong tails for balance. The basilisk lizard runs on its hind legs. Young ones can even run on the surface of the water for a short distance. Their tails help them balance. Animals that hop on two legs also have long, flexible tails. A kangaroo's tail is strong enough to support the entire weight of the animal. A kangaroo rests on its powerful tail as well as on its large hind feet, forming a supporting triangle. Fighting kangaroos leap up and kick one another with their hind feet while supporting their bodies on their tails. The tail also provides a "third leg" when the kangaroo moves slowly as it grazes. When it runs, the tail is used both for balance and steering. Jerboas and kangaroo rats are small desert mice that jump like kangaroos with the help of balancing tails.

This white tiger is using its tail for balance as it jumps.

Four-legged runners can use their long tails to balance, too. Predators like big cats must pursue fast-moving prey that zigzags at breakneck pace, trying to outrun the hunter. The cats' long tails counterbalance their weight as they make quick turns to keep up with their prey.

Squirrels use their tails for balance while climbing about in trees.

Tree-climbers need good balance and a way of responding to the unexpected bending of a branch or a sudden gust of wind. The long, bushy tail of a tree squirrel helps it balance as it runs along the branches and jumps from tree to tree. Other tree-dwellers such as lemurs and lesser pandas also have long tails for balancing, as do monkeys.

The long tail of the lesser panda also functions for balance.

Just the tip of the slow-moving binturong's tail can wrap around branches.

Hanging on is a natural use for long, flexible tails. The tails of some monkeys that live in the Americas are special. Like opossums, these animals can wrap their tails around tree branches to hang on, making it easier for them to feed on leaves almost out of reach. The undersides of their tails are bare and are very sensitive to touch. When they sleep, they anchor their tails around branches so they won't fall off if a strong wind comes up. A howler monkey's tail is so strong that the monkey can break a fall by wrapping its tail around a branch on the way down. Spider monkey tails are used just like an extra hand. If a spider monkey can't reach a desired object with its hand, it will turn around and try to grab it with the curled tip of its tail.

Tree creatures aren't the only ones that use tails for hanging on. Sea horses live among the forests of giant algae in the sea. These strange-looking armored fish coil their tails around plant strands to keep from being swept away by the water currents.

LEFT: *The naked opossum tail can wrap around tree trunks and branches.*

BELOW: *Sea horses hang onto plants with their tails.*

21

CHAPTER FOUR
TAILS THAT "TALK"

~ ~

Tails are one way animals have of telling each other things, of communicating. A white-tailed deer raises its tail straight up and wags it when running from danger, showing a bright patch of white that alerts other deer.

Animals that live in social groups may use their tails to "talk." An alarmed prairie dog swishes its tail back and forth in warning, catching the attention of other prairie dogs in the colony.

ABOVE: *Prairie dogs twitch their tails as they give an alarm call, warning others of possible danger.*

LEFT: *A white-tailed deer spreads the alarm.*

23

In a wolf pack, some animals are "dominant" to others. The other wolves are said to be "subordinate." They give way to a dominant individual. When a dominant wolf approaches a subordinate one, its tail is up. The subordinate animal keeps its tail down. This shows that it accepts the higher social position of the dominant wolf. You can see the same kinds of behavior in dogs. A confident, dominant dog holds its tail up. A shy or frightened one may keep its tail between its legs. When its owner scolds it, a dog will keep its tail down, showing that it accepts the owner as dominant.

The dominant wolf has its tail raised, while the subordinate wolf on the ground has its tail tucked between its legs.

The peacock's fan.

A male turkey, called a tom, spreads its tail feathers to attract a mate.

Some male birds and fish have a special use for their beautiful tails, attracting the attention of females.

The most familiar bird that uses its tail in courtship is the peacock. The tail feathers of the peacock are long. When he walks about or flies, the peacock holds his tail closed. But when he tries to attract a female, called a peahen, he raises his tail and fans it open. The gleaming green feathers, with their striking blue "eyes," spread out into a half circle more than eight feet across. Then the bird quivers, shaking the feathers so they make a rattling sound.

Male turkeys also spread their tails and rattle their feathers to attract mates. Male grouse stamp their feet and make a special sound in their throats as they fan out their tails during the mating season while trying to lure females to them.

The males of many bird species help raise the family. For them, the display they put on helps keep other males from their territories. The display can involve both special sounds and the spreading of feathers, including those in the tail.

RIGHT: *A raised tail is part of the grouse's mating display.*

BELOW: *An orange male swordtail displays in front of a differently colored female.*

Fish that use their tails to win females include familiar aquarium species like guppies and swordtails. The male fish swims up to the female and spreads out his beautiful tail in front of her to get her attention. Over the years, people who breed these fish have selected males with bigger and brighter tails much more colorful than those of their wild relatives.

CHAPTER FIVE
TO EAT OR BE EATEN

Some tails are used in the struggle between animals and those that would feed on them. Many mammals use their tails to swish away biting flies. Horses and zebras often help one another in this battle. They stand head to tail and brush flies from each other's faces.

Many kinds of lizards use their tails to avoid becoming a meal. The tail may be brightly colored, which attracts the attention of a predator. If the predator manages to sink its teeth into the tail of the fleeing lizard, the tail breaks off and may wriggle around, distracting the predator while the lizard escapes. The tail then regrows.

LEFT: *Like horses, zebras brush away flies for one another.*

LEFT: *Many kinds of lizards, like this American chameleon, can regrow their tails if bitten off by a predator.*

ABOVE: *The tail of the spiny-tailed dab lizard is a handy weapon. If worse comes to worse, this lizard can also lose its tail and regrow it.*

LEFT: *Porcupines' tails can inflict very painful wounds.*

The tail of the spiny-tailed dab lizard is even more useful. This lizard escapes by hiding in a crack between rocks. Then it swells up its body, jamming itself into the space, its tail sticking out behind. If the enemy keeps trying to get at the dab lizard, it swishes the spiked tail back and forth like a weapon. If the predator persists and bites, the tail comes off while the lizard stays safely in the crevice. The tail will regrow in time, ready to serve again.

Porcupine tails are very effective weapons. A threatened porcupine raises its quills and lashes out with its quill-covered tail, embedding the quills in the face of the predator. Each quill is covered by tiny, backward-pointing spines, so it is almost impossible to remove.

Predators can also use tails to their advantage. Young snakes of many species have brightly colored tails. When potential prey comes along, the snake wiggles the tip of its tail so that it looks like a worm or caterpillar. When the prey comes closer, the snake strikes. This method only works on animals like lizards or frogs that eat insects and worms. When the snake grows bigger and switches to larg-

er prey, like mice that eat plants, the tail color fades until it is just like the rest of the body.

The rubber boa has an even better trick using its tail. The boa's tail looks very much like its head. When a captive boa is released into an aquarium with a mouse nest, the snake strikes at the mother mouse's head with its tail. While she bites at the snake's tail, the snake wraps itself around the young mice and turns them into dinner. Rubber boas probably act the same way in the wild, for many of these snakes have lots of scars on their tails. The scars could come about in another way, too. When threatened by a predator, the boa coils tightly with its headlike tail sticking out. The predator could mistake the tail for the head and attack it while the boa's head remains protected within the coils.

The alligator's tail is good for more than just getting around. After an alligator has grabbed its prey, it often drags its victim into the water and hits the prey hard with its tail.

The alligator is not alone in finding its tail useful in many ways. Moving about, holding on, attacting mates, swishing away flies — these and other uses make tails very important for animals.

INDEX